DRAMA COLLECTION
WITHAM LIBRARY
18, NEWLAND STREET
WITHAM
ESSEX, CM8

30. 09. 97

GW01466578

J

15 NOV 1990

A   - 3 JUN 1991

17. 08. 95

12 JAN 1999   2 AUG 2006

- 9 DEC

21 SEP 1999

B   28 MAY 1992

3/8/00

D   18 JAN 1993

1 4 FEB 2007

05. 02. 96   2 5 AUG 2001

16. 09.

M

02. DEC 96   11·2·02

25. 04. 94

-6. JUL. 2002

06. 02. 97

26 JUN 2003   1 4 FEB 2007

05. 02. 96

15. 04. 97   1 6 SEP 2003   0 6 APR 2018

30. 09. 97

This book is to be returned on or before the date above.
It may be borrowed for a further period if not in demand.

LIBRARIES

S   — London

30130 120855779

© 1987 BY DAVID CREGAN

1. This play is fully protected under the Copyright Laws of the British Commonwealth of Nations, the United States of America and all countries of the Berne and Universal Copyright Conventions.

2. All rights, including Stage, Motion Picture, Radio, Television, Public Reading and Translation into Foreign Languages, are strictly reserved.

3. **No part of this publication may lawfully be reproduced in ANY form or by any means—photocopying, typescript, recording (including video-recording), manuscript, electronic, mechanical, or otherwise—or be transmitted or stored in a retrieval system, without prior permission.**

4. Samuel French Ltd, 52 FITZROY STREET, LONDON W1P 6JR, or their authorized agents, issue licences to amateurs to give performances of this play on payment of a fee. **This fee is subject to contract and subject to variation at the sole discretion of Samuel French Ltd.**

5. Licences are issued subject to the understanding that it shall be made clear in all advertising matter that the audience will witness an amateur performance; that the names of the authors of the plays shall be included on all announcements and on all programmes, and that the integrity of the author's work will be preserved.

    The Royalty Fee indicated below is subject to contract and subject to variation at the sole discretion of Samuel French Ltd.

6. **The publication of this play does not imply that it is necessarily available for performance by amateurs or professionals, either in the British Isles or Overseas. Amateurs and professionals considering a production are strongly advised in their own interests to apply to the appropriate agents for consent before starting rehearsals or booking a theatre or hall.**

ISBN 0 573 06477 6

JACK AND THE BEANSTALK

First presented at the Theatre Royal, Stratford East, on
1st December, 1982, with the following cast of characters:

Marge	Yvonne D'Alpra
Pam	Christine Pilgrim
Countryman 1	David John Pope
Countryman 2	Tony Armatrading
Widow Robinson	David Daker
Jack	Joanne Campbell
Milky White	Peter Durkin and David Gillespie
Mysterious Man	Jim Dunk
Cosmo	Marcel Steiner
Cosmo's Man 1	Jim Dunk
2	Peter Durkin
3	David Gillespie
Wilhelmina	Lynn Farleigh
Hen	Tony Armatrading and Susan Daly
Harp	Susan Daly

The Director was Philip Hedley
Designed by Gemma Jackson
Musical Director was Colin Sell

Subsequently presented by the New Shaw Theatre Company at the Shaw Theatre, London, in 1985, with the
following cast of characters:

Marge	Jo Warne
Pam	Tamsin Heatley
Countryman 1	Colin Harper
Countryman 2	Richard Ridings
Widow Robinson	Matthew Kelly
Jack	Vicky Licorish
Milky White the Cow	Milky White the Cow
Mysterious Man	Richard Rees
Cosmo	Martin Chamberlain

Cosmo's Man 1	Richard Rees
2	Richard Tate
3	Bill Thomas
Wilhelmina	Eve Bland
Lawyer	Colin Harper
Hen	Jaye Griffiths
Harp	Jaye Griffiths

The Director was Celia Bannerman
Set designed by Deirdre Clancy
Musical Director was Dave Brown

CHARACTERS

Marge
Pam
Countryman 1
Countryman 2
Mother
Jack
Milky White the Cow
Countrywoman
Mysterious Man
Cosmo
1st Man
2nd Man
3rd Man
Wilhelmina
Giant (voice only)
Lawyer
Hen
Harp

Prologue

ACT I

Entr'acte

ACT II

MUSICAL NUMBERS

PROLOGUE

1   No Nonsense Us   Pam and Marge

ACT I

2	My Boy's A Miracle	Mother
3	Man of Mystery	Mysterious Man
4	I Want Mother To Be Happy	Jack and Mother
5	Up The Beanstalk	The Company
6	And My Dreams	Wilhelmina
7	You'll Be On The Menu	Cosmo and his Men
8	We May Be Wicked	Cosmo and his Men
9	Gold	The Company

Entr'Acte

9a   No Nonsense Us (reprise)

ACT II

10	The Tipsy Two Step	Countryman
11	Cosmo's Lament	Cosmo and his Men
12	Lay Us An Egg	Cosmo and his Men, Wilhelmina
13	Cosmo's Dirge	Cosmo's Men
14	Measles	Wilhelmina, Cosmo and his Men
15	On My Own	Jack and Mother
16	And My Tears	Wilhelmina
17	Happy Family Hoe-down	The Company

The Piano/Vocal Score for this pantomime is available from Samuel French Ltd

PROLOGUE*

Marge and Pam enter. Marge is fat, in pale blue suit, and Pam is similar but thin, both with handbags and little hats

They are followed by three Country People. They speak the following very quickly

Marge Right. Quiet. Now. There's a farm back there and it's ours.
Pam That's right.
Marge Our trouble is, our sister and our sister's son live there but they're rotten farmers and can't pay the rent.
Pam No they can't.
Marge So we want them off.
Pam That's right.
Marge That's right. So we're sending him and him and her to take away their only cow so they'll have nothing at all and then they'll *have* to go.
Pam That's right.
Marge That's right.
Pam That's right.
Marge Speak up.
Countrymen That's right.
Marge Yes. And the whole story will be a lesson to everyone not to be poor. Right.

Song 1: No Nonsense Us

The music comes in quickly and they almost sing together

Marge		My name's Marge.
Pam		My name's Pam.
Marge		We like to barge in where we can
Pam	} *(together)*	And we get what's ours.
Marge		
	(Speaking)	No nonsense us.
Marge		We're in the right.
Pam		Oh yes we are. We're going to fight.
Marge		And what is more
Pam	\ *(together,*	We don't like jokes.
Marge	/ *speaking)* \	No nonsense us.

---

*N.B. Paragraph 3 on page ii of this Acting Edition regarding photocopying and video-recording should be carefully read.

Pam ⎱ (*together*   ⎧ We know what's what and we say so
Marge ⎰ *singing*)   ⎨ For a nickel or a peso,
                         ⎪ We'll do the deed to quench our need,
                         ⎩ With the minimum of fuss, 'cause
Pam   Her name's Marge
Marge   Her name's Pam,
Pam ⎱ (*together*)   ⎰ We like to barge in where we can
Marge ⎰   ⎱ And get what's ours.
     (*Speaking*) No nonsense us.
Marge (*straight after song*) Right, off and let's get it done.

The Countrymen and Woman exit

ACT I

SCENE 1

The Farm

To music, the Curtain opens on a dilapidated farm. A sad tree, a row of exhausted beans, a sun shining very hot. Marge and Pam move back from the front into the scene

Marge There, that's it, what's left of it.
Pam Oh, we could do it up lovely, Marge, we could.
Marge (*at keyhole*) Our sister isn't up yet, sleazy thing.
Pam A little sunshade, a few antirrhinums——

A very loud alarm clock goes off and keeps going

Marge Now you just watch how hopeless they are while we hide for a bit. (*She goes and hides near the edge of the stage*)
Pam (*joining Marge*) I'm so looking forward to getting it for ourselves.

Milky White the cow trots in. The alarm bell runs down and Milky White drops down

The door of the house flies open

Mother stands there, in kimono and snood

Mother Jack? Ja-ack? (*To Milky White*) Has he been out already?

Milky White shakes her head

It's seven o'clock, and he's supposed to be milking you like crazy. Jack?

Jack enters

Jack Here I am Mother.
Mother Just about! You're late, always late, everything's always late and it's such a lovely day as well, so good for the skin. (*She massages herself*)
Jack (*to audience*) People, Mother.
Mother (*full of charm*) Where? Oh, my lovelies! Hello. We are the Robinson family, and I am Mrs Adela Robinson, widow, and this is my lovely lad, Jack.
Jack How d'you do.
Mother And this is Milky White, our cow.

Milky White moos

And Jack's just going to do the milking so we can all have a cup of tea. (*She heads for the house*)

Jack It's no good, Mother.

Mother What isn't?

Jack You know I'll do anything for you, Mother——

Mother Oh, listen to him! (*With her arms around Jack*) Aaah! Isn't he a flower? Aaah! Now get milking while I crawl into something loose.

Jack But Milky White has no milk to give us.

Mother Just get on those udders, Jack.

Jack Mother, we're too poor to buy food for her to make milk with, so we've no milk to sell, so there's no money, so we're too poor to buy food for her to make milk with, so——

Mother (*angrily*) You said you'd do anything for me.

Jack I can't do miracles, Mother.

Mother Why not?

Pam and Marge come from their hiding place

The Countrymen and Woman enter

Marge Just give up and sell the poor beast for beef.

Pam That's right.

Mother Oh, look what's dropped in with the early morning dew. My loving sisters with their horrid little hats and handbags. Get off my farm.

Pam It's our farm.

Mother Off. Jack, see to it.

Jack Now, good morning Aunt Pam and Aunt Marge. (*He goes to them*)

Marge Don't touch us, we don't know where you've been.

Jack (*indicating the house*) Only in there.

Marge Exactly. A proper muck heap. Look at these. (*She pulls the curtains down from outside*)

Mother Those are my curtains!

Pam Well there's nothing much for them to hide, is there?

Pam and Marge screech with laughter. Mother rolls up her sleeves

Mother If Jack isn't going to do it, then——

Jack (*seeing the Countrymen*) Mother, men.

Mother (*halted by this*) What? Where? Oh! Hullo, you fine upstanding lads.

Countrywoman Careful.

Marge They've come to take away your cow for beef to pay the rent.

Jack Our Milky White?

Mother (*advancing on the men*) Not our Milky White whom we've suckled from a little calf and reared to full womanhood.

Jack They shan't touch her.

Mother (*getting her arms round the men*) No, they shan't. I'm a poor lonely, persecuted, younger-than-I-look widow. Aaah!

Men Aaah!

Mother Aaah!

Audience (*urged on*) Aaah!

Men (*tearfully*) Aaah!

Mother Oh, aren't they lovely? Hearts of gold, haven't you? Eh? Hearts of gold? Aaah! (*To Countrywoman*) Haven't they, love?

Countrywoman Yes, but they're spoken for.
Man 1 We can't take her cow, missus.
Man 2 Not with her being a poor widow.
Woman She's an older woman and cunning.
Mother Never! Petals, both of you. Here. (*Giving her hanky to the Men*)
Marge Milksops. Get that cow!
Mother (*fainting all over them*) Aaaah!!
Jack You've brought on one of her turns.
Marge Pam, you get it.
Pam (*alarmed*) Me?
Marge Get it!

Milky White paws the ground

Jack She won't like this, Aunt Marge.
Pam Here, kitty kitty. There's a pretty moo.

Milky White charges and chases Pam and Marge round the stage

   Oh, the beast, the horrid beast. The fiend, the fiend. (*Etc.*)
Marge Come and help us, peasants!
Mother (*anchoring the Countrymen*) Aaaaaah!
Jack Careful Milky White! Keep your temper! Don't overdo things!
Mother Oh she's turning nasty, I can't look.
Jack Milky White!
Mother Let her be, Jack.

Milky White has the aunts cornered and suddenly charges

Jack Stop!

Milky White brakes and concertinas, just in time

   Now that was your fault, Aunt Pam and Aunt Marge.
Marge If you can milk that cow and pay the rent with what comes out, you
   can stay. Is that fair or isn't it?
Man 1 Well it do seem *rather* fair, don't it?
Man 2 It do seem *rather* fair, yes.
Countrywoman It seems very fair.
Mother All right. If that's how you want it. Jack?
Jack Mother?
Mother A miracle. Sharp.
Jack I'll try Mother. Milky White. A miracle. (*He collects a stool and pail
   from outside the front door and sits and milks. Nothing*)
Mother Nothing?
Jack Nothing?
Mother Perhaps the hole's blocked. Has anyone a pin?
Marge She's dry.
Pam She's dry.
Marge |
Pam | (*together*) So off!
Mother Oh, you're so pleased. Let an old hand have a go. Come on love lay

us a pint or two of gold top. (*She pulls several times*) Come
oooooooooooon!

*Mother pulls the udder a long way back, then lets go. It hits Milky White very
painfully. She is affected as if hit in a sensitive place, and moos*

Marge Nothing!
Pam Nothing!
Marge Nothing. So off with you.
Mother But where can I go? Fellas?
Man 1 ⎫
Man 2 ⎬ (*together*) We're engaged.
Countrywoman To me.
Mother Both of them?
Countrywoman While I'm considering, yes.
Jack I will save you, Mother. Milky White, I will take you to market and
sell you to an absolutely fabulous person who will feed you and love you
and fill you full of milk again. I'll sell you for fifty pounds, for a hundred
pounds, for two hundred pounds.
Mother Oh, Jack!
Jack I will, I promise.
Mother Oh, isn't he a peach?

Milky White looks worried

Jack And Milky White, you're not to worry because it's for Mother that
we're doing this. And when the farm's going properly again, I'll buy you
back and you shall have whatever you want.
Mother And so shall I. Oh there's a boy for you, a real boy.

Song 2: My Boy's A Miracle

(*Singing*)   My boy's a miracle,
My boy's a friend,
My boy's the best boy
That heaven could find to send.
When he comes home tonight,
My boy will be free
Of poverty, misery, heartbreak,
And he'll do it just for me,
Yes he'll do it just for me.

My boy's a wonder boy,
My boy's a king,
My boy's the one boy
To make the angels sing.
When my boy smiles at me
My world fills with joy,
He gives to me,
Lives for me always.
He's my loving wonder boy,

Yes,
He's my loving wonder boy.

All   Her/my boy's a miracle,
Her/my boy's a friend,
Her/my boy's the best boy
That heaven could find to send
When he comes home tonight
Her/my boy will be free,
Of poverty, misery, heartbreak,
And he'll do it all for me/you,
Yes he'll do it all for me/you.

Jack Come on then, Milky White. Let's go and do it.
Mother ⎫
Countrymen ⎬ (*together*) Good bye, good bye.
Jack ⎭

Jack and Milky White go

Pam (*weeping*) What a lovely tune, Marge.
Marge Rubbish. He'll never do it.
Mother He will.
Marge Let's go and see then.

Pam and Marge go

Mother Oh, he's a love!

SCENE 2

On The Way To Market

Seated on a small rock is a Mysterious Man. He has bright eyes, a beard, and a cross expression

Mysterious Man What happens now is me and I'm a Mysterious Man.

Song 3: Man of Mystery

I don't know where I come from,
And I don't know where I go;
I often don't know why I do
The things I do, and so
My mystery is total,
And that's all I can sing,
And if you do not like it
You can do the other thing.

Yah yah fiddlesticks,
Nanky poo and biff.
I am a man of mystery
And I find it bores me stiff.

What's what and which way up
I couldn't tell you if I tried,
And even when I turn it round
I don't know what's inside.
The mystery is total,
And I wish I'd stayed in bed,
And if you do not like it,
You can go and boil yer 'ead.

Bing bong Chinese gong,
Goblins on your lawn,
I am a man of mystery
And I find it makes me yawn.

Now watch today's little trick.

Jack and Milky White enter

Jack All morning on the road to market and still not there.
Mysterious Man Good morning lad. I'm a Mysterious Man. What is that?
Jack It's our cow, Milky White, and I'm taking her to market to sell.
Mysterious Man She's pretty scraggy.

Milky White is offended

Jack She's not. She's lovely. (*He begins to move away*)
Mysterious Man Just a minute. You look a bright sort of lad. How many beans make five?
Jack That's easy. Two in each hand and one in the mouth.
Mysterious Man Er—yes they do. Well done. As a reward I'll give you five magic beans in exchange for that animal.

Milky White shakes her head

Jack Five beans for a cow? You must think I'm a fool.

Milky White nods

Mysterious Man It happens that they're magic beans, young fellow, and if you plant them in your garden, wondrous things will happen, apparently.
Jack Really?
Mysterious Man Apparently.
Jack A miracle! I knew it! Done!

Milky White, alarmed, intervenes in the following

Mysterious Man Here they are then, ancient beans handed down from generation to generation. (*To Milky White*) Don't eat them!—and if you use them properly, you could become the happiest boy in the world.
Jack Oh, thank you, Mysterious Man. Mother will be pleased.

Milky White shakes her head and moos

She will, I know she will. You will look after Milky White won't you, because I'll want her back eventually.

Mysterious Man I can't think why. In the meantime, come and sit by me, cow, and be mysterious. (*He pulls Milky White to him and sings*)

> We don't know where we're going,
> And we won't know when we're there.
> It's endlessly annoying
> Just to be you don't know where.
> The mystery is total,
> It confuses me no end.
> Imagine bobbing around all day,
> With this thing for a friend.
>
> Poooh pah rumpty tum,
> Wobbly in the guts.
> I am a man of mystery
> And find it drives me nuts.

Suddenly the Mysterious Man shoots down through a trap door (or similar) with Milky White

Jack Well, good bye Milky White, hello fortune. I'll go home right away and tell Mother. She'll be absolutely thrilled.

Jack goes

Marge and Pam enter screeching with laughter

Pam She won't be able to pay her rent now.

Pam | (*together*) | The farm will be ours. (*They go into their little song,*
Marge | | *music as for Song 1*)

Marge	We don't like beans.
Pam	We don't like boys.
Marge	We don't like men.
Pam	We don't like joys.
Both	We never smile.
Pam	We never think.
Marge	We never dream.
Pam	We stuff ourselves
	With buns and cream.

Marge (*breaking out of song and going off*) And we don't like that either. Come on and get a cup of tea, I'm sweating and we've got to get back to the farm.

Pam (*following*) My feet are sharp as razor blades.

Marge and Pam exit

SCENE 3

The Farm. Night-time

Mother is laying a table in front of the house. There is a lamp on the table

Mother I'm preparing for when Jack comes home. He's been so long on the road I'll bet he's stopped to buy a treat for me—a joint of beef, some jelly and a bottle or two of this and that. Oh, I tell you, my loves, there's going to be merry-making here tonight. We'll eat beneath the stars and dance ourselves mad. I'll just go and pop into something shimmery, because I've been so nervous all day I've still got my nightwear on.

Jack (*off*) Mother!

Mother Oh, this is it, this is the moment! My boy, and even better, my money! Jack!

Jack enters

Jack Hello, Mother. What a day!

Mother Oh, look at him, glistening in the moonlight. Every mother's dream, eh?

Jack Yes.

Mother Come on, Jack, tell us the news.

Jack Well, I went towards the market all morning——

Mother Did you buy us some food?

Jack Wait. And on the way I met this very interesting person.

Mother Champagne and rissoles and chocolate bon-bons?

Jack Mother, I've got something more than food.

Mother Oh, isn't he a love?

Jack I sold Milky White then and there, to this person who was a Mysterious Man.

Mother They all are love. (*She chortles*) What did you get?

Jack Well, Mother, you'll never guess.

Mother No, I won't, tell me quick.

Jack I got these. (*He shows the beans*)

Mother What are they?

Jack Beans.

Mother Just the five?

Jack Yes.

Mother Don't pull my leg, Jack, a joke's a joke, but we're poor.

Jack It's not a joke.

Mother You mean you set off for market to make our fortune and sold our well-nurtured, thoroughbred cow for five beans?

Jack They're magic beans, Mother.

Mother They're what?

Jack If you plant them in the ground, wondrous things will happen, apparently.

Mother These aren't magic beans, these are shrivelled up rotten old beans.

Jack No, Mother, he said——

Mother There aren't any magic beans anywhere in the world.

Jack But the man said——

Mother I don't care what he said, they're just beans, mouldy beans, beans you can't plant, you can't eat——

Jack But he said——

Mother He saw you coming Jacko. He saw you lolloping down the road with no more sense than that cow and he said, "There's a blistering young fool, I'll take him to the cleaners," and he did.

Jack But Mother ...

Mother You stupid, idiotic numbskull of a boy. You halfbaked adolescent layabout. You've taken all we ever had in the world and you've sold it for five beans, five *beans*—oh isn't he a fool? Beans, I mean beans, that's probably all he's got in his head is beans. He's beans from the neck up, is Jack Robinson. He's short of nothing but a brain!

Jack I thought you'd be pleased.

Mother You thought I'd be pleased when you came home with no food, no money, no cow, nothing but five crumpled up and miserable little beans?

Jack Have I done wrong?

Mother Yes, you've done wrong, about as wrong as you could do. How are we going to pay the rent?

Jack I didn't think of that.

Mother You didn't think of that because you couldn't think of that. You're stupid and you've ruined us.

Jack I'm sorry Mother.

Mother You're sorry? Is that all?

Jack I'm unhappy, too. Very unhappy.

Pam and Marge enter

Marge But we're not.

Pam We're pleased.

Marge Very pleased.

Mother And come to gloat, no doubt.

Pam ⎱
Marge ⎰ (*together*) Yes.

Mother Well, get out and leave me to my misery.

Marge (*leaving*) It's the lawyers now, Pam.

Pam (*leaving*) It's the lawyers now, Marge. They'll get the farm back for us.

Marge And don't expect charity, just because we're sisters.

Marge and Pam exit

Mother I don't expect anything any more, ever! Who'd have children, eh, who'd have kids? (*She wanders tearfully to the back*)

Song 4: I Want Mother To Be Happy

Jack (*singing*)   I want Mother to be happy,
                              I want life to come true,
                              I want to be warm,

> In an old-fashioned home
> With old-fashioned things to do.
> I want dinner in the larder,
> I want friends to come and play,
> But the very best thing
> That my wanting could bring
> Is to take my Mother's pain away.

Mother

> I want lolly by the thousand,
> I don't want to sweat and rush,
> I just want to dance
> Through a lifetime romance
> In a world that is pink and plush.

Jack

> I just want to do the right thing,
> I just want to help all day.

Mother
Jack } *(together)* {
> But the very best thing
> That our wanting could bring
> Would be taking all this pain away.

Mother goes to Jack, takes the beans and throws them away. She sits outside the house

Jack exits into the house

The Lights fade to a Black-out

SCENE 4

The Farm. The next day

Music starts for the growing of the beanstalk. The beanstalk comes up through the trap on something like a chimney sweep's brush, wobbling around, so that it can be attached to the beanstalk on the flies which will be used later

Gradually, the light changes to day and the sun appears. When the transformation is complete, and a really thick, ropey beanstalk has appeared, the alarm clock goes off

Mother leaps awake

Mother Jack! Jack! It's seven o'clock. You're supposed to be milking like crazy. (*She sees the beanstalk*) Aaaaaaaaaagh! JAAAAAAAAAAACK! Something terrible has happened!

Jack comes out of the house

Jack Here I am Mother.
Mother We've been taken over by a great Thing!

Jack sees the beanstalk, and puts his arms around Mother

Jack It's the beans!
Mother It often is but I didn't have any last night.

Jack He said they were magic beans, and they are. Wait there. I'm going to seek our fortune, and it's all going to be all right! (*He starts to climb*)

Mother Jack, come back. I need you! You're all I've got, Jack. And I love you!

Jack has climbed to about roof height and the set is removed. The beanstalk begins to come down into the trap, so that he can now pretend to climb it at stage level as it slowly unrolls

As Jack climbs, a few birds come in and fly around him. Then a large gas balloon floats past him, preferably with someone in the basket. An aeroplane passes at the back. A vulture and some little fluffy clouds—all these start high and end low as he goes up. The moon, very surprised passes and finally a very huge cloud comes down covering the whole of the aperture. The music goes on, and when the huge cloud sinks to the ground level we come out the other side, and into Scene 5

SCENE 5

The Giant's Garden. Huge rose bushes and flowers all about; across the back is a vast washing line

Jack steps off the top of the beanstalk, perhaps now at the side

Jack What an adventure! I wish Mother had come.

Voices (*off, shouting*) Let's get the laundry up, then. On with the Giant's laundry.

Jack I think I'd better hide until I'm sure I'm safe. (*He hides behind one of the bushes*)

Three men bring on ladders and a big basket

Men (*together*) Right, the Giant's laundry, the Giant's laundry, Cosmo said we must put up the Giant's laundry.

1st Man Your turn up the ladder.

3rd Man It's always my turn up the ladder.

2nd Man That's right.

1st Man One Giant's sock.

2nd Man One Giant's sock.

3rd Man One Giant's sock.

Jack A Giant. I'd like to see a Giant.

1st Man One Giant's string vest.

2nd Man One Giant's string vest.

3rd Man One Giant's string vest.

1st Man Move the ladder.

3rd Man Let me off, I get giddy.

2nd Man Hold tight.

3rd Man Oh, my head, my head.

2nd Man There we are, it didn't fall off, did it?

1st Man One Giant's handkerchief.

Jack I'll hide in his laundry and then we'll meet face to face or something to something. (*He hides in a sock*)

1st Man Move the ladder.

2nd Man Hold your head.

3rd Man Oh, oh, I'm going to be sick.

2nd Man No, you're not. Swallow it. Where's the other sock?

3rd Man There's always only one sock in the laundry.

1st Man One Giant's night cap.

2nd Man One Giant's night cap.

3rd Man One Giant's night cap.

1st Man Oh, there's the other sock. (*It contains Jack*)

2nd Man Perhaps it's full of Giant's toenails.

3rd Man Or perhaps some of his gold.

2nd Man Let's look.

They crowd round

   Cosmo enters

Cosmo And what are you all about, my merry men?

Men Nothing, Cosmo. Hanging up the Giant's laundry, Cosmo, ever so busy, Cosmo.

Cosmo Well, I'm a horribly suspicious man, and at the moment I am more than usually horribly suspicious. For one thing, there's someone out there.

They all peer at the audience

Men Yes, Cosmo, so there is Cosmo. (*etc.*)

Cosmo You out there, this is Giantland, and I am Cosmo, the Giant's dwarf. I am the biggest dwarf in history. Though on occasion I can go small.

1st Man Show 'em Cosmo.

2nd Man Go on, Cosmo.

3rd Man Be a little Cosmo.

1st Man Little and horrid.

Cosmo Shall I? Right.

Cosmo pulls back his coat and reveals shoes on his knees, onto which he drops instantly pulling horrid faces and making horrid noises. The others applaud. He silences them with his hand

   D'you know what it is that's out there? It's boys that's out there. Boys, lads, rows and rows of nice growing boys. The very thing the Giant likes to eat best.

1st Man Yes, he's a big boy eater, Cosmo.

2nd Man Eats 'em for snacks.

3rd Man For main course.

1st Man And for afters.

Cosmo A shelf, too. I can see a shelf of nice ripe boys, all ready to go down slippery slope with a few hard boiled eggs.

1st Man Shall I get the boy nets, Cosmo?

Cosmo No, get the Giant's night cap and we can catch them in that before they run away. There's girls, too. He likes them in his tea, and sprinkled on his Marmite butties. Oh this is going to put him in a good mood with us, this is. Now are you ready?

They spread out the Giant's enormous night cap one at each corner and bring it down

Jack escapes from the sock

One, two, three and . . .

Jack pushes the men under the cap

Jack exits

Men (*shouting together, under the cap*) A boy, a boy! There's one loose up here! I'll get him! (*etc, etc.*)

Cosmo turns

Cosmo Stay there, men. I'll deal with this. He must be in the sock. (*He runs back to the now empty sock and dives into it with a great noise. Silence. The sock with Cosmo inside stands up*)

4th Man Did you get him, Cosmo?

Cosmo No, did you?

Men No.

Cosmo Well, keep very quiet and we might catch him.

There follows a creep round the stage, the men under the night cap, and Cosmo in the sock. They stick swords out and wave them hopefully, narrowly missing each other until they finally collide. This is best done genuinely unable to see

During this, Wilhelmina, the Giant's wife, tall and thin in black, with a bun, comes on. It is possible the men catch her

Wilhelmina Cosmo, stop playing games.

Cosmo Oh, it's old lemon face.

Wilhelmina My name is Wilhelmina, and I am the Giant's wife, and I want to know what you have done with my husband's laundry.

Cosmo (*a bit sheepishly*) We've been catching boys.

Wilhelmina He doesn't want boys today, he wants spaghetti. So leave me in peace, and take the night cap to the wash again.

Cosmo Me?

Wilhelmina You.

Cosmo She's a terrible person this—she's got pins in her corsets, nettles in her bed, drinks vinegar—(*He drops to his knees suddenly, pulling faces*)

Wilhelmina Oh really. Dwarfs. Go and tell the Giant to wash his hands for lunch.

Cosmo All right. But I'll be back later with the boy nets, so don't go away, my little dears.

Cosmo and Men go

Wilhelmina All right. You can come out now.

Jack enters

Jack Thank you very much for not giving me away. Those men really wanted to eat me.

Wilhelmina They're like that. Every boy in the place goes into the stew pot for my husband and I haven't got a single one of my own to play with.

Jack How awful. In the place I come from children are loved and looked after by their mothers.

Wilhelmina Really? Do you have a mother?

Jack Not with me.

Wilhelmina Aaah! Poor thing. Come here.

Jack (*approaching nervously*) Actually, I'm very hungry at the moment, because I didn't have breakfast.

Wilhelmina Aaah! (*She grabs Jack*) No mother and no breakfast. Aaah!

Wilhelmina rocks Jack in a vast embrace. He wriggles free

Now don't run away. I'm being kind.

Jack Yes, I can see that. Do you have any food by any chance?

Wilhelmina Come and sit on my knee.

Jack I'm too hungry for knee sitting, really.

Wilhelmina If I give you some food, will you sit on my knee then?

Jack Well, I might.

Wilhelmina Oh, you're just what I'm looking for, you are.

Song 6: And My Dreams

(*Singing*)

> A little boy I never got
> To feed with milk and bread,
> To wipe his nose and smack his bot,
> And tuck up safe in bed.
> I've never ever known the thrill
> Of being called a mum,
> If you were mine I'd love you 'till
> The cows came wandering home.

> I wish I had a boy of my own,
> Of my own,
> I'd cuddle him and see he was fed.
> My heart is a heart and it's not made of stone,
> But my dreams are stuck inside my head,
> And my dreams, and my dreams, and my dreams
> Are stuck inside my head.

> In the bath I could wipe away his tears,
> From stingy soapy suds,
> And poke about inside his ears
> With cotton woolly buds.

> I wish I had a boy of my own,
> Of my own,
> I'd cuddle him and see he was fed.
> My heart is a heart and it's not made of stone,
> But my dreams are stuck inside my head,
> And my dreams, and my dreams, and my dreams
> Are stuck inside my head.

Wilhelmina grabs Jack by the hand and leaves

SCENE 6

The Giant's Kitchen

A large table protrudes from one side. There are ovens on the other side. All come about half way up the proscenium arch. Big pans are on top of the ovens on hot plates. There is a pulley up to the table top which is operated from the table top. There are rope ladders up to the hot plates and to the table top

Only Jack and Wilhelmina are there. Wilhelmina takes Jack to a stool

Wilhelmina There my precious, sit down and I'll get you some bread and milk. (*She goes to get it*)

Jack runs forward to the audience

Jack The Giant's castle! (*He glances at Wilhelmina*) But it's a bit complicated with her here.
Wilhelmina (*with bread and milk*) Come and sit down.
Jack I can eat standing up.
Wilhelmina Sit down!

Jack does. He eats and drinks

There. Now, when everyone comes in for lunch I shall pop you in to the left hand oven over there to hide. That one's quite cool so you'll be safe. (*She strokes Jack's head*) Ever so safe. (*She strokes harder*) Safe as safe as safe as safe as safe as——
Jack Please stop it.
Wilhelmina Up here, mothers stroke their children.
Jack I'm not a child.
Cosmo (*off*) Ready with the boy nets!
Wilhelmina We don't want boy nets in here, Cosmo. It's knife and fork duty, and quickly please.

Cosmo and the men enter. They have a huge knife, fork, mug and plate

Cosmo (*to audience*) After lunch, then. We'll go boying after lunch, so don't run away.

Wilhelmina stands in front of Jack and backs him round to the correct oven

Wilhelmina Get the knife and fork and the mug ready. And make sure the pulley is working.

Jack hops into the oven, which shuts with a clang

Cosmo What was that?
Wilhelmina I was looking to see if the pudding was ready yet. Whose turn
   on the table?
1st Man Mine.
Wilhelmina Up you go then.

*1st Man climbs up to the table top. 2nd and 3rd Man prepare to pass the knife
and fork up*

2nd Man Is the knife sharp?
3rd Man Yes.
2nd Man Fork pronged up, is it?
3rd Man Yes.
2nd Man Right Cosmo.
Cosmo Right, knife and fork ready for the ascent?
Men Ready, yes, yes, ready.

Much clanking as they go up

Cosmo Have you got them?
1st Man Yes. I've got them.
Cosmo Right then, mug and plate coming next.

They go up

   (*To the audience*) Look your fill. There's one or two of you will be making
   that journey before long. Ha ha ha! You, and you and you—and maybe
   one or two little girls eh, baked in custard?

Meanwhile Wilhelmina has gone up the ladder to the hotplates and calls out

Wilhelmina Get a bowl out of the bottom oven, someone. No! Not the left
   hand one, the right hand one.

Jack is peering out of a vent in the left hand oven

   That's right. Use an asbestos glove.

*The oven is opened. There is a blast of heat and light, and a bowl is pulled out
with tongs*

   Right. Leave it there and stand clear. Here's the spaghetti. (*She tips a
   saucepan and great white ropes of spaghetti fall into the bowl*)
All (*together, variously*) Well aimed. Good shot. Good for you.
Wilhelmina Stand by for the sauce.

Again the hot oven is opened. Another great bowl is pulled out

   Put it ready. (*She pulls another saucepan to the edge. It has a great bung.
   She produces a hammer*) Right. Stand clear! And—away! (*She knocks out
   the bung and a great jet of sauce pours into the bowl*)
Cosmo Right. Now get it over to the pulley.

The men hook the sauce onto the pulley

Song 7: You'll Be On The Menu

All (*singing*) This is the way we lay the table,
This is the way we lift the grub,
If we don't do what we are able,
The Giant will tickle us with his club.

Up with the sauce, so hot and luscious,
Up to the top to feed our friend,
If we should drop it he would push us
Into the pot and that's the end.

Chorus Fee fie crabalocka pie,
Winkin', blinkin', twinkle of an eye,
Work, and work, and work till you die,
Or you'll be on the menu!
(*Repeat*)

Cosmo (*speaking*) Right now, the spaghetti. Right? Right?
All (*as the spaghetti goes up*)

This is the way we lift spaghetti,
Sticky and hot as the Giant likes,
If we should spill one strand you bet he
Wouldn't half clobber us with his spikes

Chorus

This is the way we lay the table,
This is the way we lift the grub,
If we don't do what we are able,
The Giant will tickle us with his club.

Chorus

Ha ha ha ha ha ha ha ha
You'll be on the menu.

The spaghetti reaches the top, tips and falls, if possible on Cosmo

Cosmo You fools! You idiots! (*He goes on his knees and makes faces*)
Men (*together, variously*) Sorry Cosmo! Didn't mean to Cosmo! Just a
mistake Cosmo! Don't worry Cosmo!
Wilhelmina I'm not cooking any more. Shovel it up!
Men Spades! Shovels!

All dash round. The bowl is lowered

2nd Man Yuk. It tastes mucky!
Cosmo Everything he eats tastes mucky to us. He has superior taste buds
and to him it's nectar. Come on, get it into the bowl.

Much oohing and aahing and "Ow it's hot!" Up it goes

3rd Man Stop! You've left a shovel in it.

Cosmo You daft thing. Lower it again. You have to do everything yourself, here.

Cosmo reaches in when it descends, gets shovel but his hat goes in. Up it goes

Hey, my hat!
1st Man Don't worry Cosmo. I'll find it!
Cosmo I don't want him eating it.

Sudden thuds of footsteps in the distance

1st Man Right. He's washed his hands.
Cosmo Everyone ready for boot duty.

The Men stand under the table. Wilhelmina stays on the oven top. Cosmo is in the middle of the stage. The sound of the Giant's footsteps goes round the theatre and with it the sound of him saying

Giant (*off*)   Fee fi fo fum,
                    I smell the blood of an English man.
                    Be he alive or be he dead,
                    I'll grind his bones to bake my bread.

A great shadow and thud as the Giant sits in a chair, and the scraping of the chair, and then a hand falls on to the table. Cosmo goes up the ladder and peers up. 1st Man also peers up

Cosmo Good morning, sire. How is it up there?
Giant (*off*) I smell boy.
Cosmo There's a good crop of them out here, sire, and we're going to get the boy net after lunch and——
Giant (*off*) Boy in the kitchen.
Wilhelmina Sire! Sire!
Giant (*off*) Wife?
Wilhelmina It's the one you had last night, sire, the one grilled in butter. The smell is still about.
Giant (*off*) Oh.
Wilhelmina Now eat up your spaghetti like a good Giant.
Giant (*off*) What?
Wilhelmina (*curtseying*) I mean would you like to eat your spaghetti, sire?
Giant (*off*) Soon.
Cosmo Who's a silly lemon face?

Wilhelmina puts her tongue out discreetly

Giant (*off*) Boot off.
Cosmo Of course, sire.

A foot comes in under the table and falls on the 2nd Man. Cosmo descends half way to supervise boot pulling

(*Calling*) Could you lift it, sire? Small accident, sire. Only a broken back, but it's inconvenient.

The booted foot is lifted

Thank you, sire.

2nd Man (*wriggling free but funny shaped*) I shall never be the same again.

Cosmo Just take an aspirin in a glass of milk and you'll be fine.

Giant (*off*) Boot off!

Cosmo Yes, sire. At once, sire. Pull. Pull. Pull.

The men under the table pull away and get the boot off, displaying a steaming sock. They totter away

Giant (*off*) Massage!

Cosmo comes down

Cosmo Yes, sire.

Cosmo nearly faints, then puts on a gas mask. He uses a rake to tickle the foot. Great giggles. The foot moves around and finally pushes Cosmo away. He goes up the ladder in the gas mask. As he comes to the top, great screams off

Giant (*off*) Monster.

The hand goes up and nearly knocks Cosmo off

Cosmo (*taking off the mask and reappearing*) I'm sorry to frighten you, sire, but perhaps you should eat before your spaghetti gets cold

Giant (*off*) Yes. And get my gold.

Cosmo Sire.

Cosmo comes down as the 1st Man puts spaghetti on a fork and into a hand which goes up and comes back empty during the next bit

Go and get his gold. He always likes to count it after lunch.

The Men on the floor go and get it

Wilhelmina is now on the floor too. She is peeping round to look for Jack

Got something special there for pudding?

Wilhelmina It's not for you. Have a ham sandwich.

1st Man (*from above*) Psst. Psst.

Cosmo I must say you're a bit cautious with our rations, Wilhelmina.

Wilhelmina I have to work to make ends meet, like everyone else.

1st Man Psst!

Cosmo Oh what is it?

1st Man We've forgotten the wine!

Cosmo Oh—they're so careless.

The fork hand comes down without spaghetti

Giant (*off*) More spaghetti!

1st Man One moment, sire. Have you got it, Cosmo?

Cosmo rolls a keg of wine to the pulley and attaches it

Cosmo Yes. Wind up.

The wind-up starts. Cosmo munches a sandwich

Giant (*off*) More spaghetti!
1st Man Oh, all right, sire.

The keg was nearly up. 1st Man lets go. The keg descends and Cosmo, either caught or holding on with one hand goes up

Cosmo Help! Quick! Come and get me!
1st Man Sorry Cosmo. I didn't mean to Cosmo. (*He dashes back and lowers Cosmo*)
Giant (*off*) More!

The hand moves about impatiently

1st Man runs to the fork. Cosmo goes up again

   2nd and 3rd Man enter with gold bags, see Cosmo and rush to relieve him, dropping gold

Wilhelmina munches sandwiches and watches throughout

Men (*together, variously*) Oh Cosmo! How terrible Cosmo. We'll get you down Cosmo. (*etc.*)

Jack comes out of the oven

Jack (*to audience*) Gold! Just what Mother and I need.

   Jack takes a bag of gold and goes

Wilhelmina There. That'll teach you to interfere, you silly dwarf.

Cosmo, free, drops to his knees and pulls faces

   Oh, give over.

A second forkful has gone to the Giant

2nd Man Cosmo. Cosmo. You won't like this Cosmo. Someone's taken some gold.
Cosmo Someone's what?
Giant (*off*) This lot of spaghetti's foul! Foul! Foul! Foul!

Spaghetti comes as if spat from the Giant's mouth. With it is the remains of Cosmo's hat

Cosmo My hat!
Giant (*off*) My gold!
Wilhelmina My boy!

All rush around

Cosmo (*to rushing assistants*) Never mind his gold, look at my hat!
Wilhelmina (*having run to the oven*) Oh, the rascal. He's gone. My plaything! My boy! (*She stamps her foot*)

The Giant bangs the table and shouts "Gold!" incessantly. The assistants run about

Cosmo comes forward and the frontcloth falls behind him

Cosmo I'm not going to let you see the scene that's happening there. First of all the Giant clobbered us all.

Shrieks off

And then he pulls us into little bits.

Cries of "Ooooh! Aaaah! Help!" come from behind the Curtain

And then he stuck us together again.

Cries of "Oh! Goodness! How funny! You've got my foot haven't you?" etc. come from behind the Curtain

And then there was trouble over his laundry.

Giant (*off*) My knickers, Cosmo!

Cosmo And then we got him to sleep in a special way we have which is a very deep secret.

The Giant snores

And after all that we sang this short ditty, which I wrote myself.

The Men appear, limping and with arms in slings

Song 8: We May Be Wicked

All   We may be wicked——
                          Well, yes, we are
                          All of us swear and how we cuss.
                          But none of us had a papa or mama,
                          So don't think too badly of us.
                          Not of us.

Cosmo See you later with the boy nets.

The Men go off

Note: Some productions may have difficulty making the scene changes at this point. In that case, Cosmo can cover with the following speech

Cosmo (*to audience*) While they go off to lick their wounds—lick away, laddies, lick away—there is something you might like to know about the Giant's eating habits. He doesn't just like the chubbier children, the ones that go pop between his finger and thumb. He likes the long and stringy ones as well. He likes them especially because they get caught in his teeth, and the flavour lingers in his mouth all day long. Then he prods them with his toothpick. (*He chuckles*) Sometimes these stringier children get caught in among his big gnashers at the back, and he gets his finger nail, like this, and he has a good old poke about until he finds them. If they get caught in that niggling little gap at the front, he gets his shirt front, which is none too clean, and has a thorough wipe-up, like this. The ones that go straight down are much better off because they're drowned, most of them, before they get past his tonsils, and then they get dissolved very quickly in his huge rumbling tum. I'll be off now, but don't worry, because I'll be back to demonstrate some of these delightful habits of his when I return with the boy nets. All right? 'Bye.

Cosmo goes

Jack enters

Jack Don't worry, we're going back to Mother, and we're going with the horrid Giant's gold. Won't she be thrilled!? What an adventure!

Jack runs off

SCENE 7

The Ruined Farm

The beanstalk has grown like a giant tree and can be a cut-out at this stage. It spreads all over and has things dangling on it

Marge and Pam stand there facing a lawyer

Marge Look at it, Mr Lawyer.
Lawyer It's amazing.
Marge It's a mess. It spoils the view and it's on our land.
Pam That's right.
Marge And the house is a mess.
Pam The roof's a mess.
Marge The window's a mess.
Pam The furniture's a mess.
Marge The crops are a mess.
Pam The soil's a mess.
Marge And the biggest mess of all——
Marge ⎱
Pam ⎰ (*together*) Is her.

    Mother enters, very dejected

Pam Adela!
Marge Adela!
Lawyer Mrs Robinson.
Pam ⎱
Marge ⎰ (*together*) Listen to us!
Mother (*to audience*) I'm so worried about Jack. I want him home.
Marge You've got to come and have things explained.
Mother I've lost my son up a beanstalk so clear off.
Pam We've a lawyer here, Adela.
Mother Are you single?
Lawyer Er——
Mother I'm looking for a husband you see, mainly for Jack, if the poor boy's still alive. (*Near tears*) He's getting funny.
Pam He's no good.

Mother He's the best that ever was and I miss him. (*Slight tears*)
Lawyer Aaah!
Mother But it isn't right to go galivanting up a beanstalk when we're in trouble.
Lawyer Perhaps he meant it for the best.
Marge Now don't you go soft on her as well. (*Calling off*) You two. Come in here and show us your bills. She owes pounds and pounds and pounds, this woman.

A Countryman and Woman enter

Countryman We'm found your cow, missus, wandering about all dazed like.
Countrywoman Yes, all dazed like.
Mother You mean Milky White?
Countryman \
Countrywoman } (*together*) That's her, that's the one, (*etc.*)
Marge The bills, the bills.

Milky White enters

Mother Oh, Milky White, my love, my precious, it's no good coming home duck, we've nothing to feed you on. Take her away, and give her a meal.
Countryman For you, missus, anything.
Countrywoman Eh, she's found a man, look.
Lawyer Oh dear, oh dear, oh dear, surely something will turn up.
Pam \
Marge } (*together*) Us.
Mother There is nothing left, Mr Lawyer, love, flower. All we can hope for is a good marriage or pennies from heaven.

Gold coins fall onto the stage

Did you do that?
Lawyer No.
Mother Then who did?

Jack drops down the beanstalk with a bag in his hand

Jack I did Mother, I did.
Mother Jack! Oh Jack, you're safe and sound (*She embraces Jack*)
Jack And I've a whole bag of gold, Mother, look.
Pam \
Marge } (*together*) Gold?
Countryman \
Countrywoman } (*together*) Gold?
Lawyer Gold?
Mother Never mind that, Jack, it's you that matters. (*She gives him another hug*)
Lawyer Aaah. She's very sweet, you know.
Mother Did you say gold?
Jack Yes, Mother, we'll never be poor again, and Milky White shall have a golden cow shed and everything's turning out just as we dreamed.

Pam That's torn it, Marge.

Marge Just smile and be nice for a bit. It's not over yet.

Mother has been scrabbling in the bag during the above and now stands up

Mother It is gold. I'm unbelievably rich, steaming, stinking, filthy rich! (*To Pam and Marge*) So stick that in your curlers and frizzle it.

Song 9: Gold

ALL   Gold, gold, gold, gold, gold, gold—
        Gold!
        There's nothing quite so good as gold!
        It makes you happy when the world is grey
        It takes your cares away.
        And keeps you gay
        And never old.

        Because it's
        Gold!
        There's nothing makes you quite so bold!
        It keeps you happy through the night you know,
        And keeps you smiling so
        You'll grow and grow
        To heights untold.

        It gives you life,
        It keeps you free
        From horrid strife
        Uncertainty.
        It makes the whole world seem a perfect place
        And bursts out in
        Your laughing face.

        Because it's
        Gold!
        The only warmth against the cold.
        It stifles all your sorrows, all your sighs,
        And what it's not, it buys.
        In all our eyes there's nothing
        Quite so good as gold!

The last verse is reprised

CURTAIN

ENTR'ACTE

Marge and Pam enter

Marge Right, Act Two, put away your crisps and listen.
Pam That's right.
Marge They've done it again.
Pam That's right.
Marge Spent up.
Pam Spent up.
Marge Done up the farm, new cow shed, lots of silly nonsense.
Pam Quite pretty, they say.
Marge *BUT*—have they paid their bills?
Marge ⎫ (*together*) No, they haven't
Pam ⎭
Pam Can they pay their bills?
Marge ⎫ (*together*) No, they can't.
Pam ⎭
Marge So, here we go again.

Song 9a: No Nonsense Us (reprise)

Marge ⎫ (*together*)		We aren't fools
Pam ⎭		
Pam		We know what's what.
Marge		We know the rules
		And what we've got
Marge ⎫ (*together*)		We always keep.
Pam ⎭		
		· No nonsense us.
Marge		That's our place
Pam		And what is more
Marge		It's a disgrace...

(*breaking out of song as before*)... that we aren't living in it at this moment, so let's get in, get on and get it over with quick and no messing.
Pam That's right.
Marge You lot, it's taking away the cow again! Where are they?
Pam It's taking away the cow again, yoohoo! Have you gone ahead?

Marge and Pam exit

ACT II

SCENE 1

The new, super farm: all coloured lights and Tudor bits and a bar, an ice cream machine and a gold cow shed and a chaise longue

Coloured lights round the bottom of the beanstalk

Mother is there in very smart clothes indeed. The two Countrymen are there too, well away with drink. One is talking to Mother and one is feeding whisky to the cow

Mother (*to the men*) So, I said to the Mayor, I said "Pull your own chain, I said and (*Seeing the audience, she detaches herself, and speaks to them*)—"Ow! Hello, my lovelies. Isn't it all terribly desirable, my little place in the country? (*More like the Mother we know*) Oh, we have such a lot of fun now we're rich—new this, new that, we don't know where to put it all. (*With confidence*) And I think we might have spent a bob or two more than we meant, but what's money for eh? In fact, (*moving back*) these two were sent by you know who to take the cow again but I don't think they can remember.

Marge and Pam enter

Marge You men!
Mother Hi, sister. Come to have a look at my development?
Marge (*angry at men*) What are you drinking?
Countrymen (*drunkenly*) Dandelion and burdock.
Marge You're supposed to take away the cow.

Milky White rolls over and blows bubbles

Mother I don't think she's going to get taken anywhere just now love, so what about a freshener while you're here.
Pam Oh, I'd love a small glass of sweet sherry, Adela.
Marge Pam!
Pam Well, it's so nice, Marge.
Marge It's common and it's not paid for.
Mother (*arriving with drinks*) There we are and I've spiced it up just a teeny tiny bit.
Marge (*producing a great pile of bills*) Adela, I have collected all these bills from the unhappy townspeople you have not paid. I have also added in the rent you still haven't paid to us. As a result I have to say, you owe us all about——

Jack enters, very busily

Jack Mother, we need a tractor.
Mother Oh, do we dear?
Marge You can make do with a hoe for now.
Jack Oh? (*Seeing the bills*) What are those?
Mother Jack, just come over here and keep cool with some ice cream, will you? I've things to say.
Marge That's it. She's going to send him up the beanstalk again.
Pam Oh!
Marge And this time I'll bet whoever it is up there will be waiting for him.
Pam Oh, Marge.
Marge It's not your fault if he gets eaten, Pam. And without him she's lost. Sup up, and get me one.
Jack I don't believe you've spent it *all*.
Mother No, I haven't, not all, but quite a lot of it has sort of gone. So why don't you go up there and get some more?
Jack It's dangerous.
Mother That's all part of the fun.
Jack Mother, just give me the keys of the safe, so I can get what's left of the gold, pay the bills and get back to my planting.
Mother You mean these?
Jack Yes, those. And get that cow the right way up.

Jack leaves

Countryman 1 She's making Irish cream for Irish coffee.
Mother Oh blow it, he's going to have a go at me, now. Well, let's keep cheerful while we can. Are you all right, loves? Missing that fiancée of yours, are you?
Countryman 1 No.
Countryman 2 No.
Countryman 1 Never given her a thought.

Song 10: Tipsy Two-Step

All sway to their feet, saying they're fine and sing the soft shoe shuffle song that follows

All

> We might be just a little bit tiddly,
> An eensy weensy tiny bit slewed,
> Our legs are feelin' funny,
> We got wobbles in the tummy,
> And we 'opes you'll beg us pardon bein' rude,
> But we 'as to admit we'm stewed.
>
> We're feelin' just a woosy bit airborne,
> A floatin' with the fairies far away,
> We're just about aware that there is somebody out there,

But who they are and what they does we couldn't say,
'Cos we're all out for the day.

Dance

And ooh—the feelin',
That oosy woosy boosy floosy feelin',
We're on the ceilin',
From where we stand
Life is grand.

And we may be just a little bit wobbly,
An itsy witsy teensy bit oiled,
We feel that we were fated for to be inebriated,
But underneath it all we'm still unspoiled,
Yes, we 'as to admit we'm boiled.

We're muddled,
Befuddled,
We're tipsy,
We're dipsy,
We swilled it,
We swigged it,
We soaked it, we pigged it,
We drained the cup,
Then filled it up,
And now we're off our food,
But we 'as to admit
That we're feelin' just a bit,
Yes we 'as to admit
We'm STEWED.

With Milky White they do a soft shoe dance, Mother joining in

Mother Oh, you're loves, all of you, loves of the first order.

Jack enters with an empty bag

Jack It's completely empty.
Mother What?
Jack We've no money left. We've spent everything.
Men On dandelion and burdock?
Marge Aha!
Pam Thank you for doing it up. Now go.
Marge Now go.
Mother I will not! Jack is just going to the bank. (*She points up*) It's so much
    fun for him.
Marge Aha!
Pam Oho!
Jack All right, Mother. I will "go to the bank" as you call it—one last time.
    Aunt Marge and Aunt Pam?
Pam Who?

Marge Us?

Jack I will have the money for you tonight. (*To Mother*) And as for you, I'm ashamed of you.

Mother Of me?

Jack You've wasted everything and made us look very foolish in front of everyone.

Mother is open-mouthed at his cheek

(*To the Countrymen*) While I'm away, I expect you gentlemen to see that she behaves properly.

The Countrymen mutter various promises

So goodbye for now. And be good.

Jack climbs away up the beanstalk

Mother stands with her back to it all. The men gather and wave a bit. Then there is a little silence. They turn back and look at Mother

Pam (*whispering*) He's gone, Marge.

Marge Here's hoping.

Mother turns

Mother If I've got to behave properly, at least I'm going to enjoy it. Give me your glasses, flowers, and you, too, you old thistles.

Possible reprise of a line or two of Song 10

SCENE 2

An enormous hen coop

Wilhelmina leads on an enormous Hen

Wilhelmina Hello again. This is the Giant's special hen and I have just taken her out for a little scratch. In you go. (*She pushes the Hen into the coop*) Aha! Who is this? (*She hides*)

Jack enters

Jack (*to the audience*) Here we are again. I want to get some more gold and get home quick. I don't like it here, one way and another. (*He see the Hen*) Good heavens, what a huge chicken! (*He goes and peers through bars*)

Wilhelmina creeps up behind Jack and, when he turns, he turns directly into her arms and is held in a great hug

Wilhelmina Aaah! Aaah!

Jack Let go!

Wilhelmina Shall I call the Giant?

Jack No.

Wilhelmina Well I might. You ran away from me and made me feel funny inside. I think I will call the Giant to punish you.
Jack He'll eat me.
Wilhelmina H'm. I really want to keep you to play with.

Sounds of Cosmo, off

Oh that Cosmo. Get in there (*She opens the coop a tiny bit; to the Hen*) And don't you peck him or there'll be trouble.

Wilhelmina moves out of sight. Jack can't be seen at all

Cosmo enters, in deepest gloom

Song 11: Cosmo's Lament

Cosmo   (*Recitative*)
Alas poor me
I am so unhappy.
Observe a dismal dwarf.
A right sad little chappie

I have been abused—
I have been beaten by the Giant without let or halt.
And none of it——
Oh none of it—
Has been my fault.

Verdi-ish oompahs

Life is unfair,
Rotten to the core,
Bitter the taste of its berries.
Life's full of care,
And what is more
It's just not a bowl of cherries.

The three Men enter in bandages, limping

Men   Poor old Cosmo!
Torn out with worry his hair is.
Life's full of care
And what is more
It's just not a bowl of cherries!

They all repeat the song, (see Score)

Cosmo drops to his knees and pulls faces. The Hen squawks with alarm

Wilhelmina (*appearing*) You've harassed my hen.
Cosmo Oh, shut up. It wasn't me that lost the gold, and looked after that boy.
Wilhelmina No. It was me that did some of it.
Cosmo Yes. What's the Giant going to say when I tell him that?

Wilhelmina The Giant always believes his wife and I shall say that you are
lying.
Cosmo Oh, you terrible woman! Losing gold, harbouring boys, getting us
into trouble——
1st Man Let the hen out, Cosmo.
2nd Man The Giant's special hen.
Cosmo Eh?
3rd Man She's in charge of the hen, so if it escapes, then the Giant'll blame
her.
Cosmo What a good idea, out with it men. Ha ha, ha ha. Come on.

*They open the door and the Hen waddles out. Wilhelmina, unmoved by all this,
slams the door on the escaping Jack*

*Cosmo and the Men now shoo the Hen away. Cosmo gives it knees and faces,
and eventually it wanders down into the audience*

There. Explain *that* when he next wants an egg.
Giant (*off*) Cosmo, where are you?

The Giant can be heard approaching

Cosmo Here, sire, afternoon, sire, mind that oak tree, sire.
Giant (*off*) Ah. As you're there, just get the hen to lay an egg.
Cosmo Me?
Wilhelmina Yes, you.

The Giant can be heard moving away

Cosmo Are you sure he meant me?
Wilhelmina Of course he did.
Cosmo You'd better get her back.
Wilhelmina You'd better get her back.

*Much ado in the audience with the Hen, which finally sits on someone's lap,
and can't be got at*

Giant (*off*) Is the egg ready?
Wilhelmina Cosmo's lost it, I'm afraid.
Cosmo I haven't, I haven't.
Wilhelmina Will you promise to say nothing about my boy plaything if I get
it back?
Cosmo Oh, all right.
Wilhelmina (*gently*) Here, chuck, chuck, chuck.

Wilhelmina persuades the Hen on to the stage

It's all done by kindness.
Cosmo Come on then, an egg. Get ready.

Song 12: Lay Us An Egg

All   Egg, egg, lay us an egg.
                 We're here to catch it

So lift up your leg.
Don't mess about with it,
Ruffle or pout with it,
Heave and get out with it,
One great enormous
Huge dinosaurous,
Gold, gold, golden egg.

Huge whirring sounds are heard, which stop

Giant (*off*) Where's my egg?
Wilhelmina Try again. She's been over-excited poor thing.

All   Egg, egg, lay us an egg.
Not just a small one but
Big as a keg.
Make it a proper one,
Not just a copper one,
Lay us a whopper one,
Shiny and glistening,
We are all listening,
Gold, gold, golden egg!

*Sudden whirrings and great bangs and whistles interrupt the song. The Hen
gets up to reveal a big golden egg. All cheer greatly*

Giant (*off*) Cosmo!
Cosmo (*off*) Coming sire.
Giant (*off*) Ho ho ho!

The three Men and Cosmo exit in a line, singing

Cosmo and   Egg, egg, we've got an egg.
Men   We picked it up as she lifted her leg.
She didn't mess about with it,
Ruffle or pout with it,
She just got out with it,
Shiny and glistening,
We were all listening,
For one great enormous
Huge dinosaurous,
Gold, gold, golden egg

The Hen settles

Jack (*through the bars*) That was amazing. Does she always do it?
Wilhelmina You just have to say "lay" and it happens. I suppose you
wouldn't happen to be hungry, would you?
Jack Yes.
Wilhelmina Oh goody. I can't resist the idea of feeding you all on my own.

Wilhelmina rushes off

Jack wriggles out of the coop

Jack Hen, would you like to come and live with me in another place?

The Hen is doubtful

Oh, you'd love it. It's really lovely with Mother—well with me, and our farm. Here's a picture. Look.

The Hen looks. Jack gets the Hen round the neck

Right, come and lay eggs for Mother and me.

The Hen squawks. Jack puts hand over beak and starts to drag the Hen off

Giant (*off*) My hen! Someone's stealing my hen! And it smells like a boy!

Jack gets the Hen off

At the same time Cosmo and the three Men rush on shouting

Giant (*off*) Stop that boy. Arrest that boy. Bash that boy.

The Giant's footsteps approach and a huge shadow comes over things

(*Off*) Cosmo. You've lost that boy and you've lost that hen.

Cosmo It wasn't my fault. I was with you, sire. Really, if you'd just think occasionally.

Giant (*off*) How dare you!

Cosmo No, don't, please. Please! Those people mustn't see this. It's going to be awful.

The frontcloth is drawn

SCENE 3

In front of the frontcloth

Jack and the Hen run on

The usual Giant punishing noises go on behind the Curtain

Jack There, you hear that? Well, you don't want to live with people like that, do you?

The Hen shakes her head

No, so come on down with me where it's all lovely and peaceful.

Wilhelmina (*off*) Boy!

Wilhelmina comes on

Come back to be fed.

Jack No. I'm going back to my real mother. And don't follow me or I'll do something awful.

Wilhelmina But can't you have two mothers, one up here and one down there.

Jack (*leaving*) Don't be silly.

Jack goes

Wilhelmina Oh, the pig. But he'll be back. He's a greedy little fellow, though lovely, and he'll come for something else, you see. In the meantime, I'll wait. Oh.

The three Men enter, carrying Cosmo

Song 13: Cosmo's Dirge

Men   Cosmo's gone,
                     Dead as lard,
                     He wasn't much good,
                     But he tried very hard.
                     In memory fond,
                     We shed some tears,
                     We hope he can hear us—

Cosmo sits up

Cosmo   I can my dears!
(*Speaking*) Now run along after that boy, chop chop.
Wilhelmina Too late. You've let him escape again, which the Giant will note.
2nd Man The Giant's asleep.

The Giant's snores are heard, off

3rd Man We have this secret way of doing that.
Cosmo Well, when he wakes up, he's going to have some nice, refreshing boys to eat.
1st Man Out there, Cosmo? One or two of those?
Cosmo Yes. The boy nets, Men.

Excitement. Wilhelmina is distraught

Wilhelmina Oh dear! You all remind me so of him!
Cosmo One, two——
Wilhelmina Stop! They're the wrong sort for giants.
Cosmo Nonsense. They're nice and fat with ice cream from the interval. One, two——
Wilhelmina They've all got measles.
Men Oh, no, Cosmo, we can't Cosmo, please Cosmo, measles is awful Cosmo, horrid scabs, Cosmo.

The Men back right off into a huddle

Cosmo (*peering*) Measles?
Wilhelmina Yes. (*She urges the audience to say "yes"*)
Cosmo They don't look spotty to me. Are you spotty?

Wilhelmina urges them to say "yes" again

Oh no, you're not.
Audience Oh yes, we are. (*etc*)
Cosmo Right. We'll test them.

Song 14: Measles

> People getting measles
> Have a horrid head
> A runny, drippy nose
> And want to go to bed.
> They tickle and they prickle
> And they're jumpy as a flea,
> If you ask them how they are,
> They shout, "Please leave us be!"

(*Speaking*) Anyone feel like that?
Audience (*urged on by Wilhelmina*) Yes!
Wilhelmina I tell you what, let's see if any of them sing that song with feeling. If they sing it with feeling they've got the measles, if not, they haven't.
Cosmo Well, I don't know.

Song routine. Wilhelmina makes them sing loudly, Cosmo says they aren't singing loudly. Eventually

Men They've got it. They've all got the measles, Cosmo, they have.

The three Men leave

Cosmo drops to his knees and pulls faces then gets up again

Cosmo I'm not convinced. I'm going to get my measles-testing machine.

Cosmo goes

Wilhelmina Oh, that never works. There, in memory of the one that got away.

Wilhelmina throws sweets into audience and prances off

Scene 4

The Farm. Night-time

Fairy lights on. Moon. Lights on in cottage. Milky White is on stage

Jack and the Hen have just arrived. The Hen has her beak tied up with a scarf. It looks pretty ruffled

Jack There we are. Home. Isn't it lovely?

Good reaction from the Hen

Yes, it's nice, it really is. I'll go and find Mother. You'll like Mother. In time. (*He looks in the house*) Funny. Mother!

Jack goes off

Milky White moos. The Hen looks and looks away, hen-like and ruffled. Milky White comes and inspects the Hen and after doing so, laughs. The Hen pecks Milky White sharply in the rump. Milky White stops laughing. The Hen goes round, pecking things. Milky White, wishing to protect them, stops her as she is about to peck, say a chaise longue, and nudges the Hen away. The Hen squawks mournfully and rubs her tummy with her wings. Milky White goes and gets an ice cream. The Hen likes it and has some more. Milky White clears her throat and begins to moo the first line of the Indian Love Call *(from* Rose Marie*). The Hen, entranced, clucks the second line. Milky White moos the third line and together they draw to a sweet conclusion, after which they kiss. The Hen returns to the ice cream*

Jack enters pulling Mother by the hand

Mother Oh, I've got such a headache.
Jack I told you to be good.
Mother I was, but I got thirsty. Oh whatever's that?
Jack It's a magic hen.
Mother And where's the gold?
Jack There isn't any gold this time, there's just——
Mother What d'you mean there isn't any gold? There's got to be gold, we've got to pay the rent and the bills and buy some food.

Pam and Marge enter with the bedraggled Countrymen

Pam Ooh, my head.
Marge Right then, where's the money?
Mother There isn't any. Mr Stupid here has come back with a hen instead.
2nd Countryman That bain't be no hen.
3rd Countryman 'Tis more of a dodo.
Jack It's a hen! And it's magic!
Mother It's eating my ice cream! I'll wring your neck unless——

Jack intervenes with the aid of Milky White

Jack Mother! Stop it!
Mother You mind your language.
Jack (*settling the Hen*) She isn't like this really. You sit down and make yourself comfy.
Marge She is like this.
Pam She is.
Marge Spendthrift.
Pam Loudmouth.
Marge Bully.
Pam Drunken sot.
Pam |
Marge | (*together*) And we want paying.
Mother Jack? Tell them off.
Jack Quiet, Mother.

Mother (*upset*) But I'm not like that.
Jack No, just lay. Lay a nice, you know, yellow egg.
Mother Jack, I'm your loving Mother, not a loud-mouthed, bullying——
Jack Shush Mother!
Mother Don't shush me——
Marge Where's the cash?

The whirring and banging of egg-laying start again and then stops

Mother There's something wrong with that.
Jack Do shush.
Mother Hens do not make noises like that under normal circumstances!

More noises. The Hen gets up—another egg has been laid. There is much applause and amazement

Jack (*holding it aloft*) There you are. Solid gold. Thank you *very* much.

Milky White and the Hen nuzzle

Pam It *is* gold, Marge.
Mother Oh, Jack, Jacky, Jack Jack! That is a miracle. (*She hugs Jack*)
Pam Marge?
Marge It's on our land so it's our hen. (*She grabs the Hen*)
Mother (*pulling the other way*) It's not your hen, it's my hen.
Marge It's mine.
Mother It's mine.

And so on for a bit

Jack (*separating them*) She's not yours and she's not yours. She's ours!
Mother Who planted those beans? Who knew the best bit of soil?

"It's mine. It's mine" resumes

Jack Oh, stop it all three of you. You make me sick.
Mother Jack!
Jack I've done everything I can for you Mother, and all you want is more.
Mother Jack!
Jack And you too, Aunt Pam and Aunt Marge. You're nasty, greedy women.

There is uproar

You can say what you like, because I'm leaving you, now, this minute. I hope you're happy squabbling like children because I feel the call to be really grown up. I'm going to go away to find a new life for myself.
Mother You can't go now, I need you.
Jack Well, I'm sorry.

Song 15: On My Own

(*Singing*)   I must go
                 On my own,

Open skies
Stretch before me.
Wayward winds
Turn the tide,
The swallows high—
Flying o'er me;
As I sail
From your arms,
All I feel
Is the longing
To be free,
To be me
On my own.

So let me go,
Wish me well;
Fortune's spell
I must follow.
Like the sun
I have found
I am bound.
For tomorrow;
As I sail
From your heart,
All I feel
Is the hunger
To be free,
To be me
On my own.

Mother (*descant*)

Stay with your mother,
Don't you remember
All the things that I have done for you, Jack?
Scrimping and saving,
I never gave in,
God knows there were times when I was flat on my back.
Who will bake your bread,
To keep you well and fed?
Who'll comfort you when I am gone?
I can't believe
That you would leave me on my own.
All on my own.

Jack leaves

Mother Jack! Jack! (*Tearfully*) Oh dear, I'm that upset. Here (*She throws the egg to the Countrymen*) Take this and keep the change. Kids, they're nothing but trouble.

Mother goes into the house

The Countrymen leave

Pam and Marge look at the Hen, guarded by Milky White

The Hen and Milky White then leave

Pam There was a lot said then, Marge.
Marge Nasty family rows. We'll wait till morning and then we'll do what
we have to do.
Pam What's that?
Marge I don't know yet.

Pam and Marge go into the house

The Lights fade to a Black-out

SCENE 5

In front of the Curtain

Cosmo enters with the three Men

Cosmo (*to the audience*) You're still here I see. (*He chuckles*) As I thought.
Now then, I have here a measles-testing machine, and it is far more
reliable than that silly song. (*He produces a machine with two rubber pipes
sticking out of it*) So let me see. I'll take two of you young persons—a nice
savoury boy and a pleasing sugary girl and just make one final experi-
ment. Now, all you have to do is blow up one of these special balloons. If
it stays up you have measles, if it goes down, you don't.

Cosmo selects two children and gets them to blow into the machine

Oh, ho! That means you are completely free of measles. They're just the
thing to put into a boy and girl burger for the Giant when he wakes.
  And just remember as you watch them being eaten in a few
minutes——

Reprise of Song 8

The children are taken off

Jack enters

Jack (*to audience*) I'm off round the world. I'm not staying on that farm for
another minute for anyone, and I'll not go up that beanstalk again to get
money. Oh. Two of you are missing. Where did they go?

Audience reaction

What, up the beanstalk?

Audience reaction

Cosmo's taken them?

Audience reaction

That's different. I can't stand by while innocent people are eaten. I must prove my manhood, and ascend the beanstalk one more time. Then I shall show the Giant who is who!

Jack goes

SCENE 6

The Giant's Kitchen again

On the floor is a plate with ropes that can be hooked on to the pulley. Also on the floor is a huge hamburger bun which is hinged open on the audience side, so that when open, only the heads and feet of the two children can be seen

Cosmo, the two Men and the two children enter

Cosmo Right, in you go.

The children are put into the hamburger bun, the top left open

(*To the audience*) Doesn't that make your mouth water, eh?
1st Man Shall we cook them, Cosmo?
Cosmo No, he likes to eat them raw. I think we'd better tenderize them a bit in case they're a bit tough.

The Man exits and re-enters with some bashing equipment

The hamburger bun is opened and the children are "tenderized"

Are you nice and tender now? Good, they're tender. Sweet little things really. Almost too good to eat. Now, the garnish. Got to be garnished. Onions first.

Bucketfuls of giant-sized onion rings are produced. Everyone is weeping except the children

2nd Man They aren't crying, Cosmo.
Cosmo Oh, but they've got to cry otherwise they won't be juicy and full of flavour. Here let me.

Cosmo drops to his knees and pulls faces. Hopefully the children laugh

Cry. Go on cry, CRY. (*When the children laugh*) That'll have to do I suppose. Now. Ketchup.

The 2nd Man exits and re-enters with a huge ketchup bottle

Cosmo goes up the ladder and squirts masses of ketchup down on to the children

Now, mustard.

The 1st Man produces a huge pot of mustard with a spoon. Much is applied, some to the feet

And the pepper?

Cosmo produces the pepper pot from the ladder. Clouds of the stuff; Cosmo and the Men sneeze in each other's faces, and at the children, etc.

Cosmo Lettuce.

A large lettuce leaf is laid over the children

1st Man Oh, it hasn't been washed, look.

One of the Men has slipped a huge caterpillar on his arm like a glove behind the hamburger and effects the trompe-l'oeil of it crawling up to the faces of the children

Cosmo Get it. Kill it. Don't want it nibbling at these fresh young things.

It is killed and produced all dead

1st Man What shall we do with it?
Cosmo They might like to eat it while we're waiting. (*He tears a bit off and feeds the children a substitute*) It's nice, isn't it, caterpillar. Scrunchy and juicy. A bit like boy, really.
1st Man Shall we prepare the pulley, Cosmo?

The Men go to see to this

Give us the plate to see if it works.

As they are testing this Wilhelmina appears

Wilhelmina Stop that! They've got measles.
Cosmo Not these ones. I tested them specially.
Wilhelmina But they're nice! You mustn't feed nice boys to the Giant. Oh, where's my lad? Where is he?

Jack enters on to the table top—in a beam of sunlight

Jack I'm here! Don't worry!
Wilhelmina Do something, please!
Cosmo That's her boy. Get the boy nets.

The 2nd Man does so

Jack Cosmo, I've got a present for you! For all of you.

Cosmo and whoever is with him look up. Jack flings down a huge bread roll. They fall

Quick, Wilhelmina. Quick!

Wilhelmina pulls the kids close to the oven where Jack hid in Act I. To help her, Jack drops marmalade, cornflakes, All Bran on the unhappy Cosmo, and comes down the pulley, armed with a big knife, just as the 2nd Man is stopping Wilhelmina from getting the children into the oven

Here follows the Douglas Fairbanks Jnr bit. It is a fight in which Wilhelmina and Jack are attempting to get the children from hamburger to oven, and the others are trying to get the hamburger to the plate and up to the table, while also catching Jack in the net

There are available for use in this battle a bottle of ketchup, onion rings, lettuce leaves, pepper and for final use, a pot of mustard

The hamburger should reach the pulley and get lifted a foot or two from the floor before being cut free by Jack, whizzed across to Wilhelmina who gets the children into the oven

The fight should end with a straight battle between Jack with a fork or knife, and Cosmo with a mustard spoon, and Cosmo should go into the mustard pot

At this point the Giant is heard approaching

Giant (*off*)   Fe fi fo fum
                 I smell the blood of an English man.

The Giant's shadow falls

     There he is, Cosmo! The boy, get him!
Cosmo I can't. Look at me!
Giant (*off*) Get him, get him!

The two Men rush to rescue Cosmo. Jack gets into the oven with the children

   Wilhelmina exits and re-enters pushing on a large thing covered with a gold cloth

Wilhelmina Our only hope! This is our special thing for calming down the Giant.

Wilhelmina pulls of the cover, and there is a glittering Harp with a lady attached. It flashes and does all sorts of things and also makes the loveliest sounds imaginable

The effect on the stage is to produce snores from the Giant, and his arm falls from the table. Cosmo and the Men look goggle eyed and pleased. The lady might point at people to put them into this state. Jack and the children come forward from the oven. The sound stops

Harp (*a bit Kensington*) Hullo.
Jack Hello! You're the very thing I need to calm my mother and aunts. Will you come down the beanstalk with me?
Wilhelmina No!
Harp Oh yes. I love travel.
Jack Kids! Quick. Follow the Harp to the beanstalk before anyone wakes up.

This happens

Wilhelmina I want to keep all three of you. I want a family.
Jack I'm sorry, we've all got mothers of our own.

   Jack, the children and the Harp go

Wilhelmina (*to others*) Wake up! He's taking the Harp. I want my three children, I do, I do, I do!
Giant (*off; waking*) Cosmo? COSMO!

Much apology from Cosmo as general noise starts all over again and the Curtains are drawn. It would be good to have a glimpse in the half-light just before the Curtains come to, of a cut-out head with flashing eyes as the Giant leans in. A thrill for a second

SCENE 7

In front of the Curtain

Jack and the children push on the Harp

Bangs and thuds are heard off stage

Jack This way, quick. They'll follow us when he's finished punishing them.

Wilhelmina enters

Wilhelmina Come back to me!

Harp Why don't you come with us, Wilhelmina, and leave that silly old Giant?

Wilhelmina (*superior; loyal*) It may seem a funny thing to say, but in my way, I love him.

Cosmo (*off*) I know a short cut, sire. Follow me.

Giant (*off*) Right!

Running sounds are heard off stage

Jack Quick. We've no time to lose.

Harp Oh, how thrilling. Goodbye, Wilhelmina, goodbye.

Jack and the Harp go

Song 16: And My Tears

Wilhelmina (*quietly*)
> It was nice to have other people here
> For the funny things they said.
> If I could I would shed a tear
> But it's stuck in the middle of my head.

Chorus

> I wish I had a boy of my own, of my own,
> But I'll manage with a husband instead.
> He's gone where he's gone to be all on his own,
> And my tears are stuck inside my head.
> And my tears
> And my tears
> And my tears are stuck inside my head.

SCENE 8

The Farm. Early morning

The alarm goes and Milky White appears

The door flies open and Mother enters

Mother Jack! You're supposed to be milking like crazy. Oh. I'd forgotten. He's left me, Milky White.

Milky White nuzzles Mother

I've been such a silly, boring old woman, I deserve to be left on my own.

Milky White nuzzles Mother's back

Oh, that's ever so relaxing. Perhaps we'll manage then, eh?

Pam and Marge enter

Marge Right then, where's our hen?
Mother Oh clear out, you gormless oaf, she's just on the nest.

Sounds from the beanstalk start, but especially a thud, which interrupts Mother

What on earth was that?
Marge (*to Pam*) Go and look.

Pam goes off to look

Giant (*off; in the distance*) Get him!
Cosmo (*off*) *Could* you watch where you put your feet, sire?
Jack (*off*) Get the axe, Mother, the axe.
Mother It's Jack! He's been up there again.
Jack (*off*) The axe!
Mother Oh yes, Jack, certainly Jack, whatever you say, Jack.

Mother rushes into the house

Jack and the children come on down the beanstalk

Pam pushes the Harp on

Jack Did that Harp get broken when it fell?
Harp No, I'm just perfect.
Marge You're turning this into a junk yard.
Jack Now, kids, you get back to your seats, OK?

The children go

Giant (*off*) Hurry, Cosmo. Hurry.
Cosmo I'm doing my best.
Jack Mother, quick, bring the axe.
Pam (*looking up*) Oh, look at the size of that man.

Mother rushes on with the axe

Mother Here, Jack.
Jack Right. (*He starts on the beanstalk*)
Cosmo (*off*) Stop. Don't do that. Please. Don't.
Jack Push, everyone. Push.

They do and the beanstalk goes over. Marge alone does nothing. It goes. Then sound of the Giant whistling through the air. A thud. The whole cast shudder, twice, as he bounces

Pam A shame, really.
Jack It was the Giant. I've killed the Giant!
Mother Oh Jack! Isn't he a love? Aaah! Aaah! (*She kisses Jack*)
Harp Oh. What an attractive thing to do.

Noises off: the two Countrymen come on

1st Countryman Stop 'im.
2nd Countryman 'E's a fierce little beggar.
1st Countryman We was only comin' to see if you was all right Missus.

Cosmo enters on his knees

Cosmo I'll have you varmints for lunch! I'm the fiercest creature you will ever meet in your lives! (*He makes faces*)
Jack Get up, Cosmo.
Cosmo I can't. When I fell off the beanstalk my legs got pushed up inside.
Marge Now listen here, you're making a real mess out of our property and you've stolen our hen and you've made a hole out there the size of a sandpit——
Mother (*turning on Marge at the same time*) Oh shut up, you great booby, it isn't your property, and it's not your hen and my boy's a miracle and——
Jack Stop it, stop it!

Jack is ignored

(*To Harp*) Right, do your stuff.

The Harp makes happy noises and glowings and all are rendered happy

1st Countryman Can you marry a Harp?
2nd Countryman What about our fiancée?
1st Countryman I'd rather have a Harp.
2nd Countryman Looks uncomfy to me.
Jack Now then. There's enough land here for all of us to live perfectly happily in peace, together.
All Yes Jack, certainly Jack.
Jack We can farm it and live off it and if there's ever any quarrel this lady will make her charming noises and everything will be quiet and harmonious.
Harp I'll do my best.
1st Countryman (*in love*) I'm sure you will.

2nd Countryman Oh, honestly.

Jack And if you want a husband, Mother——

Mother I can see a husband. I can see the dearest sweetest little primrose of a husband just waiting for me.

Cosmo Where?

Mother Here.

Cosmo No. No! (*He does his faces*)

Mother Aaah! Isn't he a love? Isn't he a proper little cuddle, then? Aaah! (*She goes on her knees and hugs Cosmo*)

Jack So that finally is that. We can settle down as one big family and all live happily ever after.

Song 17: Happy Family Hoe-down

Jack

Aunts and Uncles,
Paws and Maws,
Scratchin' fierce at the family sores,
Bring 'em together and they sometimes fight,
But it's all forgotten in the fun tonight.

Some want houses,
Some want gold,
Some're scared they might grow old,
Put 'em together with a dosey-doe,
Wind 'em up and away they go.

Chorus

All

Swing your brother and swing your paw,
Arm in arm with your mother-in-law,
Spread the news all over town,
It's the happy family hoe-down.

Mother

Little old widow,
All pink with love,
For little old him,
We're hand in glove.

Jack

I've grown up it's plain to see,

Jack
Harp } (*together*)   Life's a doddle in harmony.

All   *Repeat Chorus*

Marge

I've been a wallflower all my life,
Who will make of me a wife?
A chunky rippling Mystery Man

The Mysterious Man enters

Mysterious Man   Stand aside—'cause here I am!

All   *Repeat Chorus*

Dance; then all freeze

  Wilhelmina enters

Wilhelmina   What's this place where music flows?
                    Something's stirring in my toes.
                    Why do I feel I'm home to stay?

All   'Cause everyday in the family is Christmas day.

                    Repeat Chorus

                    So swing your brother and swing your paw
                    Arm in arm with your mother-in-law
                    Spread the news all over town
                    We're all glad to be a happy hoe-down

                                CURTAIN

FURNITURE AND PROPERTY LIST

PROLOGUE

Personal: **Marge, Pam:** Handbags (throughout)

ACT I

SCENE 1

On stage: Farm set, including tree, row of beans, sun, house with curtained window, stool, pail

Personal: **Mother:** Handkerchief

SCENE 2

On stage: Rock

Personal: **Mysterious Man:** beans

SCENE 3

On stage: Farm set as before; additionally, table. *On it:* lamp, places set for two

Personal: **Jack:** beans

SCENE 4

On stage: Farm set, as before

Off stage: Beanstalk **(Stage Management)**
Sun **(Stage Management)**

Strike: Farm set, as beanstalk unrolls (Page 12)

Off stage: Birds, gas balloon, aeroplane, vulture, clouds, moon, a huge cloud **(Stage Management)**

SCENE 5

On stage: Giant's garden set, including rosebushes, flowers, washing line, top of beanstalk

Off stage: Ladders, basket. *In it:* Giant's clothes, including socks, handkerchief, vest, nightcap

Personal: **All Men:** Swords

SCENE 6

On stage: Giant's kitchen set, including part of large table, chair. Ovens. *On them:* hot plates with saucepans, one containing rope spaghetti; one, with a bung, sauce.
In one oven: bowls.
Pulley. Rope ladders. Stool. Bread and milk. Sandwiches. Oven glove. Tongs. Gas mask. Keg of wine. Rake. Ladder. Hammer. Shovel

Off stage: Knife, fork, mug and plate **(Cosmo** and the **Men)**
Hand **(Stage Management)**
Foot. *On it:* steaming sock, boot **(Stage Management)**
Gold bags **(2nd and 3rd Man)**
Spaghetti, part of hat **(Stage Management)**
Slings **(Men)**

SCENE 7

On stage: Farm set, more dilapidated than before
Beanstalk. *On it:* dangling things

Off stage: Gold coins **(Stage Management)**
Bag of gold **(Jack)**

ENTR'ACTE

No properties required

ACT II

SCENE 1

On stage: Farm set, modernized, including Tudor decorations, gold cow shed, bar, ice cream machine, chaise longue
Beanstalk. *On it:* coloured lights
Table. *On it:* drinks bottle and glasses
Chairs

Off stage: Tray of drinks **(Mother)**
Empty bag **(Jack)**

Personal: **Marge:** bills
Milky White: bubble producer

SCENE 2

On stage: Hen coop

Personal: **Hen:** egg

SCENE 3

Personal: **Wilhelmina:** sweets

SCENE 4

On stage; Farm set, as Act II Scene 1, ice cream from machine

Personal: **Hen:** scarf, egg

SCENE 5

Off stage: Machine with two rubber pipes **(Cosmo)**

SCENE 6

On stage: Giant's Kitchen set, as Act I Scene 6, including a plate with ropes for use
with pulley. Hamburger bun.
Ladder. Buckets containing onion rings. Mustard pot and spoon. Pepper
pot. Lettuce leaf. Bread roll. Marmalade, Cornflakes, All-Bran. Knife.
Net.

Off stage: Tenderizing equipment **(1st Man)**
Ketchup bottle **(2nd Man)**
Trolley. *On it:* a gold cloth covering the Harp **(Wilhelmina)**
Arm **(Stage Management)**
Head **(Stage Management)**

Personal: Man: caterpillar and caterpillar substitute (edible)

SCENE 7

No properties required

SCENE 8

On stage: Farm set, as Act II Scene 1

Off stage: Axe **(Mother)**

Strike: Beanstalk (Page 47)

LIGHTING PLOT

PROLOGUE

To open: General lighting in front of curtains

No cues

ACT I, SCENE 1

Cue 1	As scene opens and curtains part	(Page 3)
	Bring up lighting on full stage, bright exterior	

ACT I, SCENE 2

To open: General exterior lighting

No cues

ACT I, SCENE 3

To open: Exterior, night-time, apparent light source is practical lamp

Cue 2	Jack exits into the house	(Page 12)
	Fade to Black-out	

ACT I, SCENE 4

To open: Night-time

Cue 3	As music begins	(Page 12)
	Eerie lighting for growth of beanstalk, gradually changing to daylight as sun appears	
Cue 4	As Jack continues to climb	(Page 13)
	Lights change to reflect various stages of climb	

ACT I, SCENE 5

To open: Bright exterior lighting

No cues

ACT I, SCENE 6

To open: Interior lighting

Cue 5	As oven is opened	(Page 18)
	Light shines through opening until oven door is shut	

| *Cue* 6 | As oven is opened | (Page 18) |

Cue 6   As oven is opened   (Page 18)
Blast of light is repeated

Cue 7   **Giant:** (off) "I'll grind his bones to bake my bread."   (Page 20)
Giant's shadow appears

ACT I, Scene 7

To open: General exterior lighting

No cues

ENTR'ACTE

To open: General lighting in front of curtain

No cues

ACT II, Scene 1

Cue 8   As scene opens and curtains part   (Page 28)
Bring up lighting on full stage, exterior, daytime; practical coloured lights required for the bottom of the beanstalk

ACT II, Scene 2

To open: Exterior lighting

Cue 9   (if required) As Hen goes into audience   (Page 33)
Bring up houselights slightly or use follow spot

Cue 10   (if required) As Hen returns to stage   (Page 33)
Fade houselights or follow spot

Cue 11   **Giant:** (off) "Bash that boy."   (Page 35)
A huge shadow appears

ACT II, Scene 3

To open: General lighting in front of curtain

No cues

ACT II, Scene 4

To open: Exterior, moonlight and fairy lights and lights for cottage

Cue 12   Pam and Marge go into the House   (Page 41)
Fade to Black-out

ACT II, Scene 5

To open: General lighting in front of curtain

No cues

ACT II, SCENE 6

To open: Interior lighting

Cue 13	**Wilhelmina:** "Where is he?" *A beam of sunlight for Jack's entrance*	(Page 43)
Cue 14	**Giant:** "I smell the blood of an English man." *Giant's shadow appears*	(Page 44)
Cue 15	Wilhelmina pulls the cover off the harp *Harp's lights flash*	(Page 44)
Cue 16	Jack and the children come forward from the oven *Cut Harp's lights*	(Page 44)
Cue 17	(if required) As curtains begin to close *Fade lights on stage, bring up flashing lights of Giant's eyes*	(Page 45)

ACT II, SCENE 7

To open: General lighting in front of curtain

No cues

ACT II, SCENE 8

To open: General exterior lighting, early morning

Cue 18	**Jack:** "Right, do your stuff." *Harp's lights flash until peace is restored*	(Page 47)

EFFECTS PLOT

ACT I

Cue 1 When ready, as curtains open   (Page 3)
Music

Cue 2 **Pam:** "... a few antirrhinums—"   (Page 3)
Alarm clock goes off

Cue 3 Milky White enters   (Page 3)
Alarm bell runs down

Cue 4 As Scene 4 opens   (Page 12)
Music for the growing beanstalk

Cue 5 When transformation is complete   (Page 12)
Alarm clock goes off

Cue 6 Oven is opened   (Page 18)
Blast as of hot air expanding

Cue 7 Oven opened again   (Page 18)
Another blast

Cue 8 **Cosmo:** "I don't want him eating it."   (Page 20)
Thuds of footsteps in the distance, then moving round the theatre

Cue 9 **Giant:** "I'll grind his bones to bake my bread."   (Page 20)
Thud, then scrape of chair

ACT II

Cue 10 **Giant:** (off) "Cosmo, where are you?"   (Page 33)
Approaching footsteps

Cue 11 **Wilhelmina:** "Yes, you."   (Page 33)
Departing footsteps

Cue 12 **All:** "Gold, gold, golden egg."   (Page 34)
Whirring

Cue 13 During second verse of song 12   (Page 34)
Whirrings, bangs and whistles

Cue 14 **Giant:** (off) "Bash that boy."   (Page 35)
Approaching footsteps

Cue 15 Jack and the Hen run on   (Page 35)
Giant's "punishing" noises

Cue 16 **Marge:** "Where's the cash?"   (Page 39)
Short whirring and banging

Note: Music cues are only shown when they do not introduce songs

MADE AND PRINTED IN GREAT BRITAIN BY
LATIMER TREND & COMPANY LTD PLYMOUTH
MADE IN ENGLAND